T0023875

In the Wild

Practicing the W Sound

Novak Popovic

Rosen
PHONICS
READERS

Rosen
Classroom™

We walk in the woods.
The woods are wild!

What is in the woods?

There are wild plants
in the woods.

We see weeds.
Weeds are wild.

We watch worms.
Worms live in the dirt.

We watch a spider.
The spider weaves a web.

We see a wild bird.
The wild bird has wings.

Wait! What is that?

We see a wolf in the woods.
Watch out!

We know wolves are
wild animals.
The wolf walks by.

We love the woods.
What a wild world!